A GUIDE

J U D O

THROWING TECHNIQUE

with additional physiological explanations

By

Takumi Ohashi, M. D.

Originally published in Japan 1963

PREFACE

To be a true *Judo* player one must be equally proficient in both the techniques of throwing and locking, which are complementary to each other.

From this point of view, the author has, with the cooperation of Professor Yaichibe Kanemitsu, made the fullest possible use of his book *"Judo no Hongi"* in describing these throwing techniques.

I do hope this book will be made use of as a sister-volume to my *"Guide to Judo Grappling Techniques"* which has been published earlier.

The author will welcome any corrections or advice on any point in this publication.

Takumi Ohashi

CONTENTS

LIST OF ILLUSTRATIONS

CHAPTER I
Introductory Remarks

1. *Ukemi*

All *Judo* trainees must be practised thoroughly in the method of *Ukemi* (how to drop yourself upon the mat with safety).

In the case of dropping on your back, because of the heavy weight of the head (about 7-8 Kgs.), you will be liable to knock your head against the mat. Occasionally, you may even cause concussion of the brain. Therefore, you must hold your head upward with the neck strained.

When you are dropped by a throwing technique, strike the mat with both hands forming your body into the shape of a ship and holding the head and the legs upward (Fig. 1).

Fig. 1 *Ukemi*
(Dropping safely upon your back forming your body into the shape of a ship)

Several methods used are as follows:

No. 1. In the case of direct dropping back, keep the back of your hands upward, with both arms stretched without allowing the elbow joints to touch upon the mat; then strike the mat about one foot outward from your body and at the same time stretch out both legs forward and raise the body so as to look at your front belt straight with the eye with the neck strained. If, however, the position of your hands is too close to the body, the hands will

9

be pressed with the weight of the body and if the position of your hands is too far apart from the body, you will feel painful.

In the case of dropping on the back to the right side, by holding your body obliquely to the right, strike the mat with your right hand.

Any move in any other direction can be the same as for the above-mentioned method.

In the case of dropping on the back to the left side, it is quite the opposite to that of dropping to the right.

No. 2. Once you have gained sufficient experience in the art of No. 1, you can exercise the art of *Ukemi* with the body only half raised.

In the case of dropping directly back, put your hips slowly down and then strike the mat with both hands.

In the case of dropping on your back to the right side, put the right hip slowly down to the back placing the right foot in front of the left foot and strike the mat with your right hand.

In the case of dropping on your back to the left side, it is quite the opposite to that of falling to the right.

No. 3. When you are skillful in No. 2, you can exercise *Ukemi* standing up.

Fig. 2
Keep both palms inward

Once you have gained sufficient experience in this art, you will not hurt himself and you can exercise the art of *Judo* with prospects of rapid progress.

In the case of dropping forward or sideway, strike the mat with both palms kept inward (Fig. 2). If, however, the hands are kept too far apart from your body, the elbow joints will be liable to get hurt.

10

How to turn round upside down head over heels.

To turn round upside down to the right and front:

1. With both legs spread apart, move the right foot a little forward.

2. Put the left hand (fingers should be placed inwards) upon the top of a triangle whose base is made up of the distance between both feet.

3. Hold the right arm obliquely so that the little finger can touch the mat; then let it slip in between the right leg and the left arm.

4. Now, turn round upside down to the right and front by touching the head and the right shoulder slightly on the mat (Fig. 3).

5. Instantly, rise to the feet by striking the mat with your left hand.

Fig. 3
Let your head and shoulders touch the mat slightly.

To turn round upside down to the left and front:

Diametrically, this is opposite to the above-mentioned technique.

When you have become so skillful in this art in either the right or the left side technique that you can turn round upside down by putting your hand on the mat, then exercise this technique of turning upside down on a higher level by running, putting your hand upon the mat as far forward as possible.

11

How to turn round upside down on the back:

First, stand head over heels by putting both hands on the mat, and then turn round on either side of your shoulders.

It has been said that in former days a poster was put up at the *Genbukan Hall* (of *Kitoryu-jujitsu*—another school of *Judo*—training hall) in which this movement was continuously repeated a number of times (for example, 300 times or more than 400 times) during periods of cold-season and hot-season training.

In those days, soon after arrival at hall, trainees were in the habit of practising this movement until their regular lesson began.

Once you have gained sufficient experience on this movement, it will give you all the greater confidence in executing *"Kata"*—original classic form.

How to look at your opponent:

Always keep your attention on the movements of your opponent and main points of the technique.

Don't look aside loosely or hold your head too low.

2. *Tsukuri* and Kake

"Tsukuri" is the movement by which your opponent's stability is destroyed and at the same time your own body is carried on to a posture most appropriate for making a technical attack.

"Kake" is the movement by which the opponent is thrown down by taking advantage of his pulled-down posture.

Nothing could be more effective than such movements as *"Tsukuri"* and *"kake"*, which are completely harmonious to each to another.

For example: In the case of *ashi-barai* (one of the throwing techniques by which the opponent is thrown by using the foot); when you sweep his leg, if the movement of *Tsukuri* becomes loose, this technique will not be effective, even though the movement of *Tsukuri* has been adjusted at the start. This is usually because the opponent will be back to a stable stance.

12

It may be said that this also applies to the use of the Locking Techniques (*Katame-waza*).

Furthermore, even only in one technique, there are so many methods of *Tsukuri* and kake that you must select the right method according to opponent's posture, including his walking stance and the kind of technique with which he threatens you.

Several methods used are as follows:

How to disturb (*Tsukuri* or kuzushi) your opponent's balance.

1. In case the opponent is in a relaxed state, pull him forward or push him back, then his body will be placed off balance.

For use in approach from any other side, use the same tactic as the above-mentioned movements, namely, you must use this hold as soon as your opponent gets into a relaxed state.

2. Reaction power must be made use of!

If you push your opponent a little against his will, he will surely push back. At this moment, pull him down forward by taking advantage of his reaction.

To make your opponent's position unstable to his back: first, pull him forward and then push him back by taking advantage of this reaction.

Any other cases can be treated the same way as for the above-mentioned movements.

3. Make your opponent walk involuntarily.

Moving your body backward, with one hand (with the aid of the other hand), pull him forward to the level of your own shoulder, then he will be obliged to step forward.

As a result, his other leg (which had remained in back) must be stepped forward. For this reason, if you pull the opponent forward continuously so as not to give him time for stepping with the leg remaining in the back, the stability of his body will be disturbed in the same direction in which the pulling action is being taken.

In the case of back-side tactic, push the opponent continuously back, then employ the same trick as above.

Any other cases are treated the same way as for the above-mentioned one.

Moreover, in the case when the opponent steps forward (or backward), the treatment is the same as for the above-mentioned movement.

4. Make your opponent walk with large strides.

When the opponent is pulled forward, he will surely step forward intending to preserve his natural standing posture. For this reason, if you pull him (with the aid of the other hand) forward strongly and rapidly from your own shoulder by moving yourself to the back or turning your body, he will be forced to stride forward. Consequently, the opponent's body will be placed in an unstable position.

In using backward movement of this hold, push the opponent continuously to his back.

Any other cases are treated the same as for the above-described movements.

5. Stop your opponent in the middle of his walking.

If he is suddenly interrupted with his stepping, his body will become unstable because of the principle of inertia (it will be described later).

In the case of an opponent beginning to step or pulling his adversary with the intention of allowing him to step forward (described in No. 3), pull your opponent a little downward, then he will be suddenly interrupted in the middle of his stepping.

Thus by taking advantage of this moment, make his body unstable and without allowing him to place his foot securely upon the mat.

This movement is difficult to employ effectively, but you will become skillful after taking a number of exercises.

6. How to turn your opponent inward or outward while taking steps.

When he begins to step, pull him inward (or outward), then he will step with his leg inward (or outward) involuntarily.

14

At this stage, his body will become unstable.

7. How to twist your opponent's body.

In dealing with your opponent from the front:

For example, as soon as your opponent puts his right foot on the mat, with your left hand push his elbow or shoulder a little outward and at the same time with your right hand pull him to his left and front. His body will then be twisted and as a result, his body tends to become very unstable to his left and front.

In the case of the use of back-side tactic, do this:

For example, as soon as your opponent places his right foot on the mat, with the left hand pull his right sleeve down and inward (or directly downward) and at the same time with your right hand push him to his right and back (i.e. it may also be useful to push him directly sideway with your right hand). The opponent's body will thus be unstable in the region of his right and back.

8. How to upset your opponent's bodily balance by shifting from one tactic to another one after the next.

After drawing your opponent to a corner, pull him down to the corner you want; he will then easily be placed off balance.

For example: In attacking by *Harai-goshi* or *Hane-goshi*, pull him down and forward (B) after pushing him to his right side (Fig. 4).

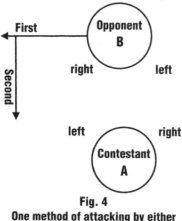

Fig. 4
One method of attacking by either
harai-goshi or hane-goshi

15

Or draw him to his front, causing him to step with his right leg (See: How to disturb an opponent's balance No. 3, page 13). Then pull him down directly forward (Fig. 5). Then his bodily balance becomes unstable.

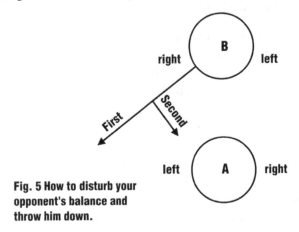

Fig. 5 How to disturb your opponent's balance and throw him down.

In case you want to apply *Hane-goshi* No. III or oh-*uchi-mata*, pull your opponent down by such action as shown in Fig. 6.

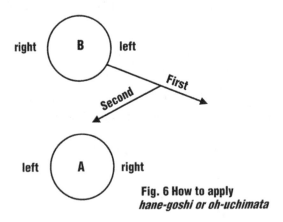

Fig. 6 How to apply *hane-goshi* or *oh-uchimata*

When applying such technique as *Oh-soto-gari*, the action of pulling him down to his right and back should be done as follows:

At first, push your opponent directly to his right and then pull him down to his right and back (Fig. 7). Or as shown in Fig. 8, first pull him down to his right and front; secondly push him down to his right and back. In other

16

words, this action is the opposite to that of *Harai-goshi* No. II or *Hane-goshi* No. II.

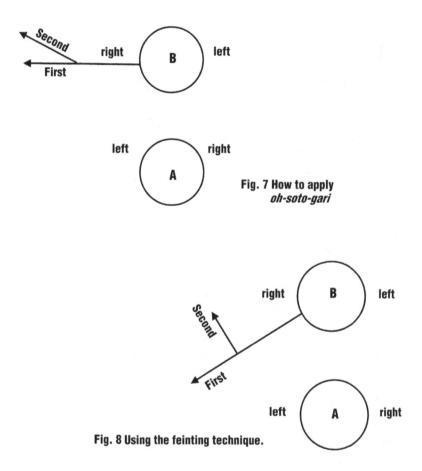

Fig. 7 How to apply *oh-soto-gari*

Fig. 8 Using the feinting technique.

To explain further, you must force your opponent to step with his right leg forward by making a feint as if you were about to pull him down to his right and front, and then you must pull him down to his right and back.

Or, by feinting as if you were about to pull him down directly to his right side, you must then pull him down to his right and back by changing the direction of your tactics (Fig. 9).

17

In another technique as shown in Fig. 10, first let your opponent step to his right and front; secondly push his body directly sideway.

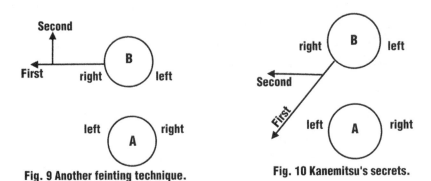

Fig. 9 Another feinting technique.

Fig. 10 Kanemitsu's secrets.

These above-mentioned techniques to throw your adversary are all Kanemitsu's secrets.

9. Essential movements in the technique for throwing down your opponent (posture to be assumed for the attack with the throwing technique) are as follows:

While pulling your opponent forward, you must step forward yourself in order to move in close to him; on the other hand, if he steps back, you must stride even further forward to move in close to him. These are the main movements by which he can be attacked with this technique.

For example: Assuming that both contestants are in their right natural standing posture, you must force your opponent to step forward with his left leg, then jerk back your right hand by placing your right foot backward.

To force the opponent to step forward with his right foot, you must pull your own left hand by moving your left leg backward.

When using this stance, even though a throwing technique is employed, it will fail if the distance between you and your opponent is too far apart to apply this technique.

Therefore, you must step forward with the leg on which you are standing (it is not the leg with which you apply the technique) and at the same time pull your opponent forward.

18

Moreover, when he steps back, you must stride with the leg (on which you are standing) far forward, carrying your body with it.

All in all, these are the essential points, and once you have gained sufficient experience in them you might practise these throwing techniques with prospects of rapid progress.

Appendix: Pertinent analysis of normal walking:

When one foot is placed upon the mat in walking, the weight of your body will gradually shift from the heel to the outer side of the sole and then to the front, and finally to the inside of the sole in rapid succession. While putting the weight of your body upon one foot, the advancing pace should be carried out with the other foot.

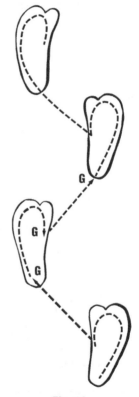

In this way the walking will proceed smoothly. In other words, the weight of the body (usually, the center of gravity of the body) will be placed either to the right or left sole alternately.

Nevertheless, in the brief instant of putting both feet on the mat while walking, the vertical line running through the center of gravity of the body will pass through the middle of both feet.

The body's center of gravity will thus move forward between the two feet in a decussate pattern.

Fig. 11
Principle of the natural walk
(how the gravity of the body shifts)

If, however, this principle of normal stepping is suddenly interrupted by some factor, the body will then readily become subject to fall. (Dr. Saburo Iino, Professor of Orthopaedics of the Tohoku Medical University in Sendai).

3. General principles of *Judo* training and method

General principles:

All *Judo* trainees should remember:

1. to apply the technique with quick motion.

2. to apply the technique fairly, eschewing dishonest practises.

3. to apply the technique vigorously so that you can show spectacular results.

How to train in the art of *Judo*.

(A) After you have achieved fundamental training, select any one of the techniques of either throwing or locking (*Katame-waza*) that you want, and then practise it in the following manner:

No. 1. In trying out a fall, forcibly repeat the same technique over and over again, even scores of times, with an opponent who is devoted only to protecting himself.

After these practice sessions, allow him to apply his revenging technique by taking advantage of chance.

No. 2. Similarly, as in No. 1, apply the technique which is connected with it.

No. 3. Exercise it so as to get the connection between techniques No. 1 and No. 2.

No. 4. Exercise it so as to grasp the relationship between throwing technique and locking technique (*Katame-waza*).

No. 5. Exercise it so as to get the relationship between your own technique and your opponent's method.

(B) Assuming that your opponent is actually there, exercise *Judo* by yourself.

Such training method as this is called by Mr. Y. Kanemitsu, "*Judo* training by yourself alone."

In the case of "*Judo* training by yourself alone", if you do not become so skilful in applying the technique that the results may justifiably be considered perfect, and if you can't apply it with the appropriate posture, then it is a foregone conclusion that you will be unable to win fighting against greater odds.

(C) Exercise "ran-dori" (*Judo* training as one pleases) in the natural standing posture, always taking the offensive without consideration of avoiding being thrown down.

In addition to all this, exercise *Judo* by changing your opponents as often as possible, and take especial care to practise *Judo* with skilful players.

In *Katame-waza* (locking technique), the same rule holds true as above.

(D) Play the game as often as possible to gain proficiency and confidence.

CHAPTER II
The Dynamics of *Nage-waza*

(The Art of Throwing)

1. The center of gravity (stable or unstable)

The center of gravity remains firm in a stable object and weakens in an unstable one—for example, when the object inclines to one side. The lower the center of gravity, and wider its base and heavier the object, more stable will it become. However, no matter how low the center of gravity and how wide the base, the object will lose its stability if a vertical line running through the centre of gravity does not pass through the center of the base.

One of the factors which determines the stability of an object depends on whether the vertical line running through the center of gravity stands on the inner side of the fulcrum O or on the outer side (see figure on next page).

In other words, the former (Fig. 12, II) is in an unstable posture but it tends to move back to stable posture through the force of restitution; the latter (Fig. 12, III) is in an absolutely unstable posture and it will finally collapse because the component forces of gravity are being exerted on the outside of the fulcrum.

When the moment of gravity (MG) resolves itself in the direction of making a right angle of the line OC which connects the distance between the center of gravity C and the fulcrum O, its component force will exert itself in the direction of the outside of the fulcrum. As a result, the object will fall.

The wider the angle $=PCQ$, (i.e. the angle between the two lines which started off from the center of gravity running to the direct opposite side of the base respectively) the more stable will the object be. In other words, the wider the base more stable will the object be. It is same with the cylinder or the cone (Fig. 12).

The cone is steady, firmly poised and sharp and yet in repose; but if it stands with its vertex in a reversed posture, it will lose its stability.

The ball is mobile, quick and elusive; but if it is forced right vertically upward, it will not be able to move by any means.

23

Fig. 12

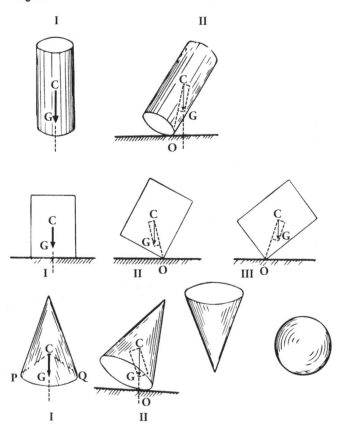

2. The moment

Fig. 13

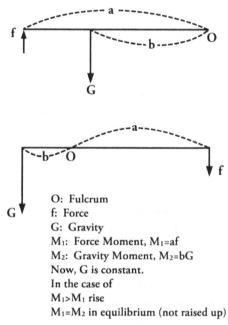

O: Fulcrum
f: Force
G: Gravity
M_1: Force Moment, $M_1=af$
M_2: Gravity Moment, $M_2=bG$
Now, G is constant.
In the case of
$M_1>M_1$ rise
$M_1=M_2$ in equilibrium (not raised up)

If the value of b is gradually increased, $M_1 \fallingdotseq M_2$, it balances and cannot rise. In other words, as the value of b is increased, more energy will be required to overthrow the opponent.

This dynamical principle of the crucial moment has been devised for practical use in leverage action.

3. The principle of the lever

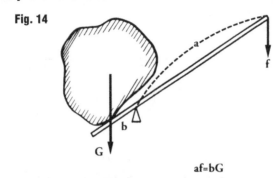

Fig. 14

$$af=bG$$

Though the object be large and heavy, you can lift it easily by using a lever. This principle of leverage can be applied in *Judo*.

For instance, in attacking with *seoi-nage* (one of the hip-throwing techniques which we shall describe later), put your hips deep into your opponent's abdomen by using yourself (especially your hips) as a fulcrum. You will easily thus be able to throw your opponent down. Moreover, it may be said that the dynamical principle used here is the same with regard to its use in *Nage-waza* (throwing techniques) or *Ne-waza* i.e. *Katame-waza* (locking techniques).

4. Energy of motion

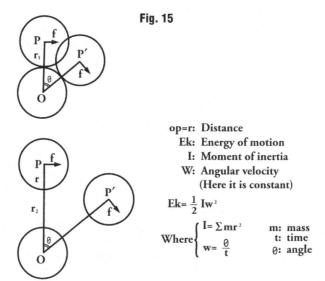

Fig. 15

op=r: Distance
Ek: Energy of motion
I: Moment of inertia
W: Angular velocity
(Here it is constant)

$$Ek= \frac{1}{2} Iw^2$$

$$Where \begin{cases} I= \Sigma mr^2 \\ w= \frac{\theta}{t} \end{cases}$$

m: mass
t: time
θ: angle

As the distance **r** is increased, more energy will be required to overthrow the opponent.

For example, in attacking by means of *Uki-goshi, Harai-goshi, Soto-maki-komi* or *Uchi-maki-komi*, etc., (these are all hip-throwing techniques which we shall describe later), you must move close in to your opponent, as close to your adversary as two plates stuck together.

Note: Beginners often fail to keep their bodies close to the opponent's hip, even when they are in a position to do so. This failure is extremely unfortunate, not only because it is undramatic, causing you to drag your opponent's body in the attempt to throw him, but also it gives the opponent a chance to attack. In other words, you will thus be vulnerable to attack by the use of *Utsuri-goshi, Ushiro-goshi* (which will be described later) and other retaliatory techniques.

27

5. The theory of inertia

When an object is under the force of some external shock, it tends to keep forever in constant motion in the direction in which the object is forced. If, however, the object is suddenly interrupted by an obstacle in the middle of its movement, it will either lose stability or finally collapse.

Proof:

When an object is moving, its Energy of Motion may be thus expressed:

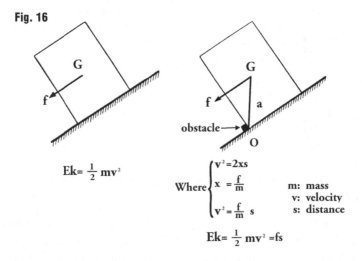

Fig. 16

$$Ek = \frac{1}{2} mv^2$$

$$Where \begin{cases} v^2 = 2xs \\ x = \frac{f}{m} \\ v^2 = \frac{f}{m} s \end{cases} \quad \begin{array}{l} m: \text{ mass} \\ v: \text{ velocity} \\ s: \text{ distance} \end{array}$$

$$Ek = \frac{1}{2} mv^2 = fs$$

If an object is suddenly interrupted by an obstacle in the middle of its movement, this Force will act upon the object through use of point **O** (the point where the object is in contact with an obstacle) as a Fulcrum.

As mentioned above in paragraph 1 "Gravity stable or unstable" (see page 23), the object will collapse as a consequence of these movements.

As far as foot movements are concerned, in attacking by *Sasae-tsurikomi-ashi* (one of the foot-throwing techniques which will be described later), let us note some pertinent rules.

The three methods used are as follows:

When the opponent's foot begins to step forward (sideway, backward); or similarly, when his foot threatens to touch the mat; or in the middle of

28

advancing one pace: In such cases, get your opponent off balance suddenly by using your foot as an obstacle.

You do this by throwing him with both your hands working in harmonized motion.

Note: Select the particular foot technique you wish to use according to the distance between you and your adversary. When we come to describing *Harai-tsurikomi-ashi* (one of the foot-throwing techniques), we shall again describe how to adjust your foot according to circumstances.

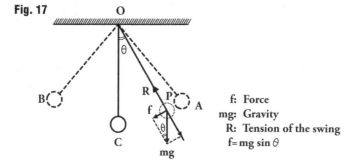

Fig. 17

f: Force
mg: Gravity
R: Tension of the swing
f= mg sin θ

6. The dynamical principle of the swing of the pendulum

When the gravity of the pendulum mg resolves itself into two forces, one of which exerts itself in the direction of the swing and the other in the direction for making a right angle of the direction of the swing, take note of the following:

Both R (the tension of the swing) and the force which occurs in the direction of the swing are neutralized one against the other. As a result, they become independent of the swing.

Thus, the width of swing depends on **f** alone.

$$f = mg \sin \theta \text{ (mg is constant)}$$

As the value of **f** (Force) is gradually increased, the angle (θ is also increased.

In other words, the stronger the force, the wider will be the swing. Moreover, the swing of the pendulum will be gradually increased by forward

29

motion and vice versa. The swing is weakened by reverse motion, i.e., such as shock against the pendulum in the direction opposite to the direction in which it is being swung.

For example, in attacking with *Okuri-ashi-barai, De-ashi-barai* or *Ko-uchi-gari*, etc, (these are all foot-throwing techniques which we shall describe later) you must follow rapidly your opponent's lead and sweep away his foot with your our own before it touches the mat. The opponent will thus be thrown.

If, however, you act against him with reversed motion, that is, in the direction contrary to his line of motion, your efforts will be useless since your act will involuntarily hold him up instead of toppling him over.

We might say here that the dynamical principle of the pendulum we described works basically in the same way when employed with other forms of tactics such as *Ashi-waza* (foot throwing techniques) or *Koshi-waza* (hip throws).

7. Couple

The overall name, Couple, is given to two forces with the same energy which are exerted on an object moving in the opposite direction, but parallel with both.

When the object is forced by the Couple, it will rotate.

We now proceed from the assumption that A's Force is stronger than that of B (A>B).

Here, the resultant force of the two factors is the difference between the two forces, i.e. (A–B).

In this case, the direction of the resultant force is the same with A and it is parallel with the two forces.

Now, the point of action of this resultant force is in the outside of that of A ($\because$A>B) where the distance between A and B (each point of action) being divided into reverse ratio of A to B in the outside of A's point of action.

Proof:

Fig. 18

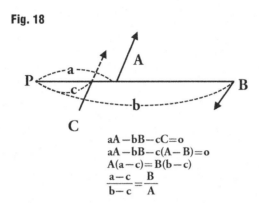

$$aA - bB - cC = 0$$
$$aA - bB - c(A - B) = 0$$
$$A(a - c) = B(b - c)$$
$$\frac{a - c}{b - c} = \frac{B}{A}$$

As a rule, (1) the direction of the resultant force is the same as that of the stronger one between the two forces of the Couple, and (2) the point of action (of the resultant force) is centered in the outside of that of the stronger force.

When both ends of the object are shocked simultaneously from opposite directions, the object will then rotate more intensively than in the case in which only one end of the object alone is being shocked.

For instance, attack him with *Ashi-waza*—foot-throwing techniques—*De-ashi-harai, Hiza-guruma* or *Osotogari*, etc.), and at the same time you must pull him down with both hands in the opposite direction to that in which his leg has been swept.

Thus your opponent will be thrown down.

CHAPTER III
Explanation of the throwing techniques

Such techniques as these are called *"Nage-waza"* (throwing techniques), by which your opponent is thrown.

There are several forms and we can divide them into five divisions: (1) *Te-waza* (hand-throwing technique) (2) *Koshi-waza* (hip-throwing technique) (3) *Ashi-waza* (foot-throwing technique) (4) *Yoko-sutemi-waza* (in applying this technique the contestant himself drops on his side, together with his adversary and (5) *Ma-sutemi-waza* in which the contestant himself drops directly on his back, together with his adversary)

Fundamental principles of the hip-throwing technique

1. Draw the body of your opponent tightly to your hip, like a pair of plates joined together.

2. With the actions of hands, legs and hips harmonized, quickly move close to your opponent as if both legs are sliding simultaneously.

Pull the hand as high as possible so as to make an acute angle between his head and your own pulling hand.

Note: Hereafter, *"Tori"* (contestant) will be represented by **A**, and *"Uke"* (opponent) will be represented by **B**.

In any case, assume that both **A** (yourself) and **B** (your opponent) are taking hold in the right natural standing posture. The explanation of the technique in the case of the left natural standing posture is quite the opposite to that of the right natural standing posture.

Uki-goshi

For carrying out this hold in the right natural standing posture, do this:

1. First, pull your opponent forward and to his right.

2. Place your left leg in front of his left toes by turning your own left foot to your left.

3. Quickly, the body is lowered (bending at both knees), and with your right arm you embrace his hips under the left arm-pit along his belt.

4. Put your right foot in front of his right foot.

5. Pull his body vigorously so as to get his abdomen and chest (i.e. his upper body) tightly upon your own hip.

6. Standing on your toes, spring up with the hips and at the same time turn to the left by pulling your left hand with the aid of the right hand.

7. The opponent will thus be thrown forward over your own right hip.

It may also be useful to leave the right hand holding the edge of your opponent's collar (*"eri"*).

Another method: At first, place your right leg in front of his right leg and then step with the left leg back to the front to his left foot. The remainder of the movement should be the same as for the action described above.

Note: Except for a little difference in the movements of hands and legs and in the maneuvering to put your hip upon the body of your opponent, the method is the same as in all other throwing techniques.

MAIN POINT:

As far as movements of hands are concerned: First, with the left hand pull your opponent's hand in a horizontal position at the level of your own shoulders. Then, for the first time, throw him down after getting his body tightly upon your own hip.

How to escape:

(1) Strain hard against him with your left hand so as to make him unable to grab your hip, by drawing your own hips downward and backward.

34

(2) Turn your own body to the right and at the same time pull your right arm back forcibly by bending the elbow joint at a right angle and keeping the wrist upward in an effort to keep it released from your opponent's left hand.

(3) Pushing his right thigh with your right hand, jump over his right leg by stepping far forward with the right leg. This technique will serve to frustrate your opponent's attack and make it non-effective (you will not be thrown).

Fig. 19 *Uki-goshi*
(First Stage)

Fig. 20 *Uki-goshi*
(Second Stage)

35

Harai-goshi

Harai-goshi No. I. Technique for use in the right natural standing posture:

1. Pushing in your right hand under your opponent's left armpit, place it on his back or grip the back portion of his jacket.

2. By means of *Tsukuri* No. 3 (see page 18), pull your opponent down to his right and front. At the same time, turn your own body to the left. Stooping low (bending the knees with the body raised), place your left leg in front of your opponent's right foot, turning your left foot to the left.

3. With both hands pull his body tightly against your own body.

4. With your right leg sweep the outside of his right leg toward his back, causing it to slip upward. At the same time, by standing on your left toes, bend your body forward quickly with hips raised. The opponent's body will thus be thrown over your right hip and then you can fling him down.

In addition, it may also prove effective to grasp his upper sleeve (or back collar) by passing your right hand over his left arm. Another method: First, let your opponent step forward with his left leg by pulling him forward and to his left; secondly pull him to his right and front when he begins to step with his right leg. At this precise moment, sweep his right leg before it has a chance to get a secure footing on the floor mat.

Harai-goshi No. II. Technique.

1. Pull your opponent forward or to his right and front.

2. With the body lowered, step with your left leg to the front of your opponent's left foot. If you are a skilful player, this might be done successfully, and his left leg will slide off by the impact.

3. Putting your right leg obliquely against the frontal lower part of his right leg, and stretching it straight as a pole, you then sweep his right leg, thus sliding it upward.

4. At the same time, turn round your own body to the left by pulling with your both hands.

By this technique your opponent will be thrown to the mat.

36

The main point and method for freeing yourself from this hold are the same as that for any other hip throws.

If you strain with both knees bent, you can loosen yourself from this hold.

Fig. 21 *Harai-goshi*

Seoi-nage

Correct method for use while in the right natural standing posture:

Fig. 22 Seoi-nage

Seoi-nage No. I. (see Fig. 22).

1. Draw your opponent (B) to his right and front and then pull up his right arm (in order to push your own right arm easily under his right arm) and place your left leg in front of his left foot by turning your left foot to your left.

2. After stooping low (by bending the knees with your body raised), turn to your left and then step with the right leg to the front of your opponent's right foot pushing your right arm under his right arm.

3. Turn your own back hard against your opponent's body by pulling his body tightly against your back.

4. Standing on your toes with both feet, raise up your hips. At the same time, pull the opponent with both hands, bending your body quickly forward, snapping sharply like a spring.

Your opponent will thus be thrown.

As a variation to this, after stepping forward with your right leg, step back with your left leg, thus throwing him. This method is also effective.

Note further: It may also be effective to apply this technique so as to shoulder the opponent by drawing him to his left and front with the right hand.

Seoi-nage No. II. Change your right hand for a grip on opponent's right collar (*"eri"*) from his left collar. The remainder of the move should be the same as for *Seoi-nage* No. I.

Seoi-nage No. III. Under the opponent's right armpit, grip the upper outside part of his sleeve with your right hand and then place his right arm deeply against your shoulder.

38

Fig. 23 *Seoi-nage* No. III

The rest of the movement can be the same as for the technique described above. (See Fig. 23).

Seoi-nage No. IV. Correct method of approach while standing in the right natural posture: In applying this technique "*seoi-nage*" against the left side of the opponent, the actions of the hand and hips are quite the opposite to the above-described movements. One point in which this technique differs from the above-mentioned ones lies in the action of the left arm, pushing your hand and shoulder under your opponent's right arm in order to grip the upper outside portion of his left sleeve at a point under his left armpit so as to make his both arms into a bundle. Then throw the opponent down by carrying both his arms upon your shoulder.

In this case, since your opponent's right arm is immobilized by your grip, this technique will prove easily successful.

It may also be effective to step forward with the right leg to the outside of his right foot, but this move will prove useless it you step in too deeply.

Additional note: Hold yourself completely set with both feet firmly in place. Then without changing your ground, turn yourself around quickly, shifting and sliding your body so that his shoulder is against your shoulder; then you thrust him down forward with a jerking movement.

In addition, for the purpose of achieving surprise and strategy in your attempt to get his body upon your right shoulder, first turn to the right, feinting as if you were about to attack his left side, and then promptly turn to your left.

Again, it is also very effective to use "*sutemi*"—in applying this technique, the contestant himself drops on his side or back, together with his opponent.

MAIN POINT:

Rotate your right wrist inward sufficiently, pushing it under your opponent's right arm; thus you will not feel pain.

39

As a result, you can draw in your own hand sharply.

How to escape:

Strain hard against your opponent's hip with your left hand, turning yourself to the right.

Note: Often it so happens that in your haste to throw your opponent, if you push out your hips too for back, your opponent's body will then become stable, being pushed back and your purpose will be defeated. For this reason, stay in front of the clapboard in your hallway; with the body raised, practise enough such fundamental training as this until you can execute the technique smoothly, without allowing your hips to touch the clapboard.

After-remarks: In attacking with *Seoi-nage* No. II or No. III, it is considered justifiable that, when your opponent's left leg begins to step forward by lifting up one or two inches, you can apply this technique more effectively than in any other case in which your opponent's right leg threatens by stepping forward. By this move your opponent cannot hook his left leg around your left leg from the outside to escape.

Usually, it is too difficult to stop suddenly, once one begins to step.

For this reason, you can apply this technique with as much confidence as you desire.

If you become skillful in using this technique in the standing posture, you can easily apply it also by putting your right knee upon the mat.

In addition, another in the throwing techniques known as *"Seoi-nage"* may also be mentioned.

However, since it is not actually very useful, we shall not describe it here.

Tsurikomi-goshi

The original form of *Tsurikomi-goshi*, known also as forming a classical pattern, is too difficult to use because it requires such elaborate theoretical explanation. Therefore, we shall not describe it here, but only the more practical version:

1. With the right hand grip your opponent's left sleeve-end (cuff) or the lower part of his elbow.

2. With your right wrist rotated outward, lift your opponent's left arm up by pulling it toward his hand.

3. Quickly move your right hip close to your opponent and then throw him down. (see Fig. 24).

Also it may also be effective to throw him by pushing his armpit, holding his arm upward. (see Fig. 25).

Fig. 24 *Tsurikomi-goshi*
(Second Stage)

Fig. 25
Tsurikomi-goshi

MAIN POINT:

The essential point here is the movement of the right arm, i.e., when his arm is raised, your own armpit must be moved up close to him.

How to escape:

Take care to forestall your opponent's hand when it threatens to lift your arm up.

Pull your elbow tightly downward so that he cannot lift it out of position.

41

Hane-goshi

In using the right natural standing posture for his hold, both contestants should take the left collar (*"eri"*) of each other with the right hand and the middle outside part of the right sleeve with the left hand.

Hane-goshi No. I.

1. Pull your opponent to his right and front. (See: *How to disturb your opponent's balance No. 3, page 13*). At the same time, draw his right arm over your own left shoulder.

2. Under his left armpit push in your own right elbow by twirling round the right wrist so as to keep the palm of the hand facing outward and the ulnar side (the little finger-side) facing upward.

Stooping low (bending the knees with the body raised), place your left leg in front of his left foot, accomplishing this by a quick sliding motion. You do this by turning your left foot to your left and holding the heel a little upward.

Fig. 26 *Hane-goshi* No. 1
(First Stage)

Fig. 27 *Hane-goshi* No. 1
(Second Stage)

4. At the same time, turn your body to the left by hooking the right leg (forming it into the shape of a Japanese syllable<) upon the front side of right leg.

42

5. Get the opponent's body tightly upon your hip so that your chin is kept covered by the upper part of his right arm.

6. Standing on your left toes, lift up his body by the hips and at the same time, sweep his right leg with your stretched right leg.

7. Tightly pull both your hands forward by turning your body to your own left. It may also be effective to grip his back collar with your right hand.

8. The body of the opponent (B) will thus topple down.

Hane-goshi No. II.

Usually, this technique is used when the opponent is relaxed in the natural standing posture.

Stooping as low as you can, throw your opponent over your own shoulder and pull him down directly forward.

In addition, throw him down by stepping far forward with him when he puts his leg behind the other foot. At this stage, bend your body to your left and front so sharply that your head threatens to touch your own foot.

Hane-goshi No. III.

Draw in your right hand in order to force your opponent to put his left leg forward. Before his left leg has been placed on the mat, sweep him to your own right and back by lifting him up with your right arm.

With regard to the positions of his feet in *Hane-goshi* No. I, No. II and No. III, we might explain here that the opponent is standing with both legs opened. If, however, when he stands with feet close together, apply the following technique:

With your right leg sweep your opponent's both legs.

You do this by hooking your leg around his both legs (lower part of the knees).

Moreover, this may also be an appropriate occasion to use the movement *"Tsukuri-kata"—(How to disturb your opponent's balance No. 2, page 13)*, i.e., at the start push your opponent to his back and then pull him down forward by taking advantage of his power of reaction.

MAIN POINTS:

(1) Pull your hand over your own shoulder, or else the body of your opponent cannot be lifted.

When his body is grasped tightly against your own hip, pull your hands downward.

(2) Lift his body with your hip and thigh.

(3) All in all, apply this technique promptly at one stroke by well harmonized action of your hands (pulling them down), and with your legs (one slipping in, the other springing over) and your hips (springing up).

Fig. 28 How to escape from Hane-goshi

How to escape and how to use the retaliatory technique (*Ushiro-goshi*).

1. When your opponent attacks from your right side, turn your own body to the right by bending your left knee.

At the same time, pushing him forward with your left hand, pull your right arm strongly to the back, causing the elbow joint to form a right angle and keeping the wrist turned upward in an effort to release it from his left hand.

2. By the experience thus acquired, you might do this: Place the weight of your own body upon the left leg, with a slight springing motion. Slightly turn your body to the right by holding the right leg upward and embrace your opponent's left flank from behind with your left arm, placing the hand upon his abdomen. Thus, you achieve your escaping technique.

3. With the intention of applying the retaliatory technique, sweep your opponent's left leg with your own left foot from his back, or sweep his left leg with your right foot by turning around yourself to the front of him.

Moreover, it may also be effective to attack by *Ushiro-goshi* or *Ura-nage* (we shall describe these later).

Notes:

44

1. In an effort to escape from his hip-throwing techniques, don't cling too closely to his body, else you will be dropped, together with your opponent (*Sutemi-waza*).

2. By means of the fundamental principles of *Judo* training, beginners must be well practised in the method "How to place the left foot in front of your opponent's left foot while stepping aside half pace with the other foot."

3. In attacking with hip-throwing techniques, consider this: Why are you liable to drop involuntarily on your back? You will fall on your back under the following circumstances:

a. If you put your left foot near your opponent's right foot in less than halfway between both his feet, even though you are in a position to place your left foot in front of his left foot.

b. Instead of standing on your toes, your left foot is placed in front of your opponent's left foot and heel, so that the weight of your body is upon the heel. As a result, your body tends to lose its stability in the backward direction.

c. If you pull your opponent downward and forward recklessly, without lifting him up, then his body will be turned to the left and it will be moved close to your own rear right.

Ashi-guruma

In employing this technique in the right natural standing posture, do this:

1. Pull your opponent down to his right and front.

At the same time, while turning yourself to the left, move your left leg to the outside of his left foot by turning your left foot to the left.

2. Hook your right leg around his right thigh, rigid as a pole.

3. Pull both your hands tightly to the left by turning round yourself to the left.

4. The opponent's body will then be thrown down with the motion of a windmill, spinning around the axis of your right leg.

MAIN POINT:

Stride up with your left leg to the outside of your opponent's left foot, at the same time pulling him down to his right and front.

How to escape:

It is the same as for the above-mentioned *Hane-goshi* and *Harai-goshi*.

Fig. 29. *Ashi-guruma*

46

Maki-goshi

This throwing technique is used in combination with *Ashi-guruma* and *Harai-goshi*.

1. First, lift up your opponent to his left and front.

2. In a manner similar to *Harai-goshi*, place your left leg in front of his left foot.

3. Hold your opponent's right hip tightly between the back of your right knee-joint.

4. Then throw him down in a manner similar to that applied in *Ashi-guruma*.

MAIN POINT:

Hold the hip of your opponent tightly by putting strength on your hip and right foot.

How to escape:

This is handled in the same manner as for *Hane-goshi* and *Ashi-guruma*.

Kakae-komi-goshi

In the case of *Uki-goshi*, you embrace your opponent's hip with your right arm. This time, however, instead of embracing his hip, with your right arm you take hold of his neck and then throw him down similar to *Uki-goshi*. Moreover, in this case, if you employ *Sutemi* (contestant himself dropping on his side together with the opponent), it will be more effective.

MAIN POINT:

With your right arm embrace your opponent's neck, keeping the back of right hand facing upward and touching the radial side (thumb side) at the neck.

How to escape:

This can be managed in the same manner as for other hip-throwing techniques. However, we advise you to hold your head downward and strain hard against his body with your left hand in an effort to prevent him from getting hold of your neck.

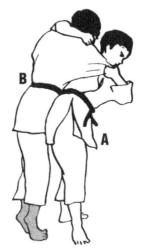

Fig. 30 *Kakae-komi-goshi*

48

Koshi-guruma

When applying a hip-throwing technique from the right side of your opponent, if your hip is being held so deeply upon the right side that his body will be crossed together with your own body, in such case as this you use this technique. As its name implies, it is called *Koshi-guruma*, i.e. hip-wheel.

In this event, needless to say, you must throw your opponent down by whirling him around strongly to your left.

Oh-goshi

In applying this technique in the right self-defensive posture, do this: Leave your right arm in the same position (pushing it under opponent's left armpit), and employ this technique in a similar fashion as that of *Uki-goshi*, by lifting him up.

Once you have gained sufficient experience in this technique, it will give you all the greater confidence in using it as one of the useful attacking techniques in a match, i.e., pushing in your right arm tightly under his left armpit and in the event he tries escaping by means of his struggles, bringing him to bay until he is taken completely off balance.

Fig. 31 *Oh-goshi*

Apply this technique at a stroke by taking advantage of his disrupted posture.

Additionally, we might explain the method of how to push your right arm under the opponent's left armpit as follows:

Thrust your right arm under his left armpit by turning round your right arm, pass it under his left arm from outside to inside, as if it (your right arm) was sliding up his left arm. (see Fig. 31).

49

Utsuri-goshi

In employing this hold in the right natural standing posture, you do so under this circumstance:

Utsuri-goshi No. I. When your opponent (B) attacks by a hip-throwing technique from your right side, do this:

How you counterattack.

1. Stooping low (bending the knees with your body raised), embrace his hip with your left arm from his back.

2. Move your chest close to your opponent, lift up his body with your both arms.

3. Instantly, get his body against your own left hip by putting his body back.

4. Then throw him down in a manner similar to uki-goshi. (see Fig. 32).

Fig. 32 *Utsuri-goshi* No. 1

Utsuri-goshi No. II. By the skilful player, this hold can best be accomplished in the following way:

Assume that your opponent attacks with a throwing technique from your right side.

50

With your body lowered, turn to the right and embrace his hip with the left arm similar to No. I, and then push him forward with your left knee and hip. At this stage, your opponent will be obliged to give up his mind to apply this technique. As a result, he will surely pull back his right hip. Taking advantage of this opportunity, promptly hold his body against your own left hip and then throw him down in a manner similar to that used in *Uki-goshi*. This move is very useful for its rationality.

Additionally, take note of this in the case of No. I: if, however, your opponent's body cannot be held tightly upon your hip in lifting him up, throw him down directly forward by means of the action of your hands (pulling tightly) and hips (springing over).

Your opponent will thus be thrown down upon his back.

Now, beginners are strictly prohibited from using such technique as this one because of its danger.

MAIN POINT:

When applying No. II, push his body with your hip and knee.

How to escape:

When he threatens to lift you up, hook your right foot around his right leg from the inside, or you might arrest his left leg with your right leg from the inside.

Ura-nage

Assume that your opponent (B) attempts to throw you by a throwing technique from your right side.

Then you attack in this fashion:

1. Stoop low; then embrace his rear hip with your left arm by placing your left hand upon his hip belt.

2. Move your left chest close to his body by holding his lower abdomen with your right arm.

3. Lift up his body to the level of your own left shoulder by holding him up with your lower abdomen and chest.

Fig. 33 Ura-nage

4. As soon as his body is lifted, promptly drop yourself on your left and throw him to your left shoulder using both hands. At this moment, his body will then be hurled down head first, as if it were a fragile article. (See Fig. 33).

Notice this: When you drop him down with this technique, withdraw your left arm to yourself, otherwise occasionally you will get hurt as a result of his body crashing upon you.

MAIN POINT:

Be sure to lift up the opponent at the level of your shoulder by holding him up with your chest and upper abdomen.

How to escape:

Strain hard against him with your right hand by bending your body forward. Or, with the intention of attacking by *Katame-waza* (locking technique), turn your hip to the right and push out your right leg to his left leg, lying yourself on the back.

In addition, this may also be a good opportunity to attack by *Maki-komi* (we shall describe this technique later).

52

Ushiro-goshi

When your opponent attacks you by means of a throwing technique, do this: Stooping low, lift his body to your front to the level of your eyes by embracing him with both arms, raising him up with your chest and upper abdomen.

Then throw him down in front of your own feet by shifting yourself to the back.

MAIN POINT:

Step back yourself as soon as your opponent is lifted.

How to escape:

In similar fashion to *Utsuri-goshi*, hook your own right foot around his right leg from the inside. You will then be able to prevent yourself from being lifted up.

Fig. 34 *Ushiro-goshi*

53

Soto-maki-komi

In employing this technique of *Soto-maki-komi* No. I in the right natural standing posture, do this:

Fig. 35 *Soto-maki-komi* No. II

1. Disrupt your opponent's balance to his right and front, by pulling your own left arm tightly in order to straighten his right arm while its middle sleeve or sleeve-end (cuff) is being held with your left hand.

2. Turn your left foot toward your own left, place your left foot on the mat and turn yourself to your left.

3. Place your right foot in front of your opponent's right foot about two or three inches away and stoop low, drawing his body in close to your own by grasping his right upper arm fully from its top with your own right arm. Then rapidly roll him down by turning yourself to your left, dropping on your back.

Soto-maki-komi No. II.

Place your left foot in front of your opponent's right little toe and then step with your right leg outward, one pace apart from your left one, by moving your own hip to the outside of his right hip. Then rapidly roll him down similarly as in No. I by taking advantage of the energy engendered by your right leg's stride forward. (See Fig. 35 and Fig. 36)

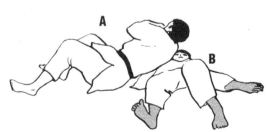

Fig. 36 The opponent is dropped upon his back by *Soto-maki-komi*

54

Uchi-maki-komi

One point in which this technique differs from *Soto-maki-komi* lies in the action of your right arm taking hold of his upper arm, embracing it from the inside (and from below).

The remainder of the movements should be the same as for *Soto-maki-komi*. (See Fig. 37).

Spin down your opponent in a fashion similar to that employed in *Soto-maki-komi* No. I and No. II.

Fig. 37 *Uchi-maki-komi*

MAIN POINT:

(1) Stretch out your opponent's right arm completely by drawing your own left hand vigorously, moving close to your opponent.

(2) Don't hold your hips too low when you roll him down.

How to escape:

Strain hard against your opponent with your left hand in order to separate yourself from him. At the same time, pull away at his right arm. He will then drop forward automatically.

Note: The above-mentioned techniques of collapsing your opponent (*Maki-komi-waza*) are the foundation of *Hane-maki-komi* and *Uchimata-maki-komi* techniques (to be described later). As a practical matter, it so happens that, even though at first you have freed yourself from him, over and over again you will be attacked by *Maki-komi-waza* (technique of rolling down).

55

Hane-maki-komi

The name *Hane-maki-komi* is given to such technique as this one, switching to *Soto-maki-komi* from *Hane-goshi*.

This technique is so effective that it has become much practised in recent years.

This is true with respect to all *Maki-komi* tactics (throwing your opponent by rolling action), but your leg action can be the same as for *Hane-goshi*, i.e., sweeping him with your leg, flinging him down by his arm similarly as in *Soto-maki-komi*.

Beginners are strictly prohibited from using this technique because of danger.

MAIN POINT:

Whirl yourself around vigorously as if you are about to rotate into the sky.

How to escape:

No hold could be more effective than the movement by which your opponent's pulling hand is forcibly shaken off, and your body is moved in a manner similar to that use in *Hane-goshi* or *Maki-komi*.

Uchi-mata

(a) *Oh-uchi-mata*

Assume that both contestants are in either the natural standing posture or the right natural standing posture.

By gripping the upper part of your opponent's left collar (*"eri"*) with your right hand and the middle outside part of his right sleeve with your left hand, place your left foot in front of his right little toe. At the same time, pull your both hands to your own right and back, together with your body, so that his stability to his left and front is destroyed (See: *How to disturb your opponent's balance No. 8, page 15*).

As soon as your opponent moves close to your own body, push your right leg deeply between his thighs, straight as a pole, so as to touch your right thigh against his right groin.

56

Tightly draw up your both hands, lifting him up, flipping him to his back with your hip and thigh. His body will then be thrown over high, your own right leg acting as an axis.

(b) *Taka-uchi-mata*

In employing this technique in the natural standing posture, pull your opponent down directly forward. Slip in your left leg inside of his left foot (if the placed position of your left foot is too far apart from his left foot, i.e., over half-way between his two feet, your efforts will prove futile).

At the same time, get at his lower abdomen with your right hip, stretch your right leg between his thighs. Lift up his body by the action of your hip and thigh.

Turn your body to the left, bend it forward and quickly pull in with your both hands. The opponent will thus be whirled down, with your own right leg acting as an axis.

A point to be stressed: When your opponent moves back, take advantage of this opportunity, and attack with this technique by throwing yourself against his body.

This technique is usually likely to be successful.

Fig. 38 *Taka-uchimata*

57

MAIN POINTS:

(1) Lift up your opponent's body by the action of your hip and thigh, i.e., you cannot raise his body with your foot alone and you must hold your leg upward momentarily.

(2) Lift up his body with your right leg, holding up his right thigh, doing this as if your own right leg were sliding quickly upward against his right leg.

How to escape and how to counterattack:

(1) When you are attacked by *Uchi-mata*, do this:

Hold your opponent's right leg between your both legs and bend back your own body, pushing out your lower belly and throwing out your chest. You can thus loosen yourself from this technique. In addition, shake loose his pulling hands.

(2) If you are a tall man, this might be done:

Springing up, hold your own left leg upward. Then turn the body of the opponent to the right by pushing his body back.

If the above-mentioned movement is done promptly at one stroke, slipping his leg, he will then be dropped automatically.

(3) From opponent's back, with your left leg sweep the leg on with which he is standing. He will then be dropped to his front.

Notes:

(1) Attacking by *Uchi-mata*, flip him down by moving tightly close to him. By such move this technique is likely to succeed. For this reason, in a situation of defence, don't cling to your opponent's body too closely or else you will be easily rolled down together with him.

(2) Beginners are often seen in using such technique as both *uchi-mata* and *Oh-uchi-gari* mixed together. But this will be of no use to them.

(c) *Ko-uchi-mata*

In employing this technique in the right natural standing posture, and with both contestants turning around to their left side as if drawing a circle,

58

sweep away your opponent's left leg with your right one. Your opponent will thus be thrown.

When you become skillful in the art of *Take-uchi-mata*, you can then also use *Ko-uchi-mata*.

Foot-throwing techniques:

1. Generally, you must exercise these techniques with the foot held rigid.

2. The technique of *Ashi-harai* (we shall describe it later) must be used with the leg stretched, and foot turned inside out.

Okuri-ashi-barai

No. I. Both contestants are in their natural standing posture: When your opponent is threatened to become unstable to his right, he will surely attempt to pull back his body to his left.

Fig. 39 *Okuri-ashi-barai*

At this stage, if you push him slightly to his left, he will be obliged to step with his left foot to the left. At this juncture you move your right leg in the same direction as his left foot, by pushing him to a corner.

Pull him to his left so as to describe a circle with him, with your left sole held stiffly (especially, the external malleolus-side). Sweep forcibly the outside part of his right ankle (whose leg at this point begins to step to the left following after his left leg). The opponent's body will thus be thrown down flatly, like a pancake.

In the event his balance is disrupted to his left due to the action of your hands, he will be thrown in the opposite side (right side).

In your use of this technique in the right natural standing posture, throw him down by breaking his balance to his left and back.

No. II. This technique is used by forcing your opponent to step to his left and front, i.e., when he is threatened with a pull-down to his right, he will certainly react to it to prevent being pulled down to his right. At this stage, for the purpose of forcing him to step to his left and front, lift him up in that

60

direction. He will then naturally begin to step with his left leg. At this juncture, turn your body to the right by placing your right foot close to the left one and when the opponent begins to step with his right leg, sweep his right foot with your left foot in a manner similar to that of the above-mentioned movement.

MAIN POINTS:

(1) Making use of your total body, pull the opponent down by moving tightly close to him.

(2) One of the essential points is the action of your straining foot used to sweep his foot. By means of dorsal-flexure of the big toe and plantar-flexure of the other toes, your foot will then be held stiffened and strained.

How to escape:

In an effort to put out your opponent's foot, hold up your own leg a little by relaxing it. This allows your opponent's foot to pass through. When this happens, sweep it (opponent's passing foot) in the same direction. This technique may be called "*Ashi-barai-goshi*" (to revenge on *Ashi-barai*).

Remember to bend your body forward and pull in both your hands by straining against your opponent.

If you are adept in the art of *Ashi-barai*, you can charm on-lookers with some really spectacular attraction.

Harai-tsurikomi-ashi

No. I.

(1) In case both contestants are standing close to each other face to face, and in the right natural standing posture (each one taking the left collar with the right hand and the middle outside part of the opponent's right sleeve with the left hand), and when your opponent begins to step with his right leg after having stepped forward with his left leg; then you attack:

Keeping the palm-side of your right wrist facing upward, with your right hand pull your opponent to your own left (at this stage, turn your face to the left and at same time pull right hand, drawing it to your own right ear or chin).

On the other hand, pull him up by drawing your left hand to the level of your shoulder.

Simultaneously, hold your right heel slightly upward, place your right foot close to the inside of your opponent's left foot so as to put your lower belly upon his lower belly.

Then turning your body to the left, sweep his right foot with your left sole as if sliding it across his right instep from below and upward, and with the aid of the right hand pull the left hand parallel with the belt.

In this way your opponent will be toppled and rolled over, like drawing a circle in the sky. This technique is appropriately employed against a tall adversary.

(2) In the case of both contestants standing and separated to a certain extent, use this hold in this manner:

Instead of placing your right foot close to the inside of your opponent's left foot described in (1), move your right foot to the outside of his left foot and then with your left sole sweep his right foot that he has placed lightly upon the mat after having stepped forward previously (See Fig. 40).

(3) When both contestants are in their natural standing posture and separated from each other to a medium extent, do this:

By placing your right foot in front of your opponent's left sole, sweep his right foot in the midst of his stepping action.

62

Fig. 40 *Harai-tsurikomi-ashi*

In case the placed position of his right foot is not too far apart from your own left foot, and when you are assured that his right foot will not step far forward, sweep his right foot at the start of its stepping process similar to No. I (1), or sweep his lightly placed right foot in a manner similar to No. I (2).

The above-mentioned explanations are only employed against your opponent's forward-stepped foot. But when this technique is employed against an adversary whose foot begins to step back, use the technique similar to that used in No. I (1); similarly, when it is employed against the foot which has been placed lightly upon the mat after stepping back, use this technique in the same way as in No. I (2).

Assuming that you sweep your opponent's right foot with your left foot, do this:

With the intention of forcing him to step with his left leg, push your right arm forward. He will then be obliged to step forward with his left leg. Right in the middle of his stepping, draw him to his right and front. (See: *How to disturb your opponent's balance No. 8, page 15*).

Pulling your both hands vigorously downward, sweep his right foot with your left sole in the same way as No. I.

He will thus be thrust thrown down to his right and front.

MAIN POINTS:

1. Sweep his foot by stretching and holding your leg rigidly, straight as a pole.

63

2. Put strength and tension in your foot by way of dorsal-flexure of the big toe and planter-flexure of your other toes.

3. Sweep your opponent's foot with your sole by turning the foot inside out.

4. Forcibly whirl around your own body, pushing out your lower belly.

How to escape:

When your opponent attacks you with this technique, by pulling both your hands tightly downward you can jump high or far away over his foot with which you are threatened with attack.

These maneuvers should provide a good opportunity for attacking with *Ashi-barai-goshi* (to revenge oneself on *Ashi-barai*). Now where should the stepping foot be placed?

If your opponent (B) is taller than you or when two contestants are standing close face to face, move your right foot to the inside of his left foot.

If both contestants (A and B) are of the same height or separated apart to a medium extent, place your right foot in front of his left foot.

If he is shorter than you or when both contestants are separated to a certain extent, step with your right foot to the outside of his left foot.

Sasae-tsurikomi-ashi

Instead of sweeping your opponent's foot, drop him down by slapping at his leg with your sole about three inches up his heel.

This is one point in which this technique differs from *Harai-tsurikomi-ashi*. The. rest of the movement should be the same as for *Harai-tsurikomi-ashi*.

Usually, this technique is applied against an opponent's right leg that is just beginning to step forward after having been held back, as well as against an opponent's right leg, and this is done with your left sole striding forward and your right leg stepping to the outside of his left foot.

Deashi-harai

Assume that both contestants are in the right natural standing posture. No. 1. You proceed as follows:

Pursuing your right leg placed backward, your opponent will step forward with his left leg.

At this point, make a feint as if you are about to step back with the left leg, instead move your left foot back a little. In the meanwhile, let the opponent step with his right leg further inside than that of the common run by pulling your own left arm inward. (See: *How to disturb your opponent's balance No. 6, page 14*).

With your opponent's right foot lightly placed upon the mat, and your left foot turned inside out, rapidly sweep the lower outside part of his right ankle-bone sideway, or sweep his heel toward the toes by pulling your left arm directly downward with the aid of your right arm, which is used to push down your opponent's left shoulder. His body will thus be slapped down on the mat as fiat as a plate (See Fig. 41).

Moreover, it may also be effective to draw your left arm inward by lifting up his body with your right arm. Or, by making use of the fundamental movements on how to attack with a throwing technique against your opponent, set up his posture in an appropriate way so that you can sweep easily his front-placed foot with your own left foot.

65

Fig. 41 *Deashi-harai*

No. 2. By loosening his pulling hands after drawing him to his left and front, his body tends to become unstable to his right and back.

Take advantage of this opportunity; attack him with this technique, similar in execution as in No. 1.

MAIN POINT:

The actions of your left arm and left foot must be completely harmonized.

How to escape:

This is a good opportunity to use *Ashi-barai-gaeshi.*

When your right foot is attacked by the left foot of your opponent, escape from his left foot by turning your right foot a little upward or backward as if it were about to draw a circle; and then sweep his left foot from the outside by pulling both your arms downward. He will consequently be dropped decisively. This technique may be called *Ashi-barai-gaeshi* (revenging on *Ashi-barai*).

66

Ko-uchi-gari

No. I (1). Assume that each one is taking hold in the right natural standing posture, and both contestants are moving.

In the case of your opponent (B) starting to step forward with his right leg, decoy him positively.

When his right foot is lightly place upon the mat, step in with your own left leg between both his legs by turning the foot to your left.

Bend your body forward. Then with your right foot sweep the upper part of his right heel so that his right foot slips across the mat. At this juncture, pull your left arm downward, push him down to his right and back with your right arm. He will consequently be dropped upon his back, flatter than a pancake. (See Fig. 42).

Fig. 43 *Kouchi-gari* No. I (1)

In addition to this, in executing your leg-sweep, it may also be effective to push away his left arm to the outside with your right hand, and this move is usually likely to be successful in conjunction with your attempt to sweep his right leg with your right heel.

When both contestants are standing close together, pull your opponent tightly in order to force him to step far forward with his right leg; when you accomplish this, move your own left leg back until his left toes touch your right heel.

Stoop low, pull him down by drawing the left hand around to the left and back parallel with your belt. Then push from his inside to the outside with

67

your right hand. Then he will lose his stability. At this moment, sweep his right heel with your right foot.

No. I (2). When sweeping, embrace his right flank with your right arm, keeping the palm of your hand facing to his front (i.e., the little finger side—ulnar side—is kept upward). Then push him down by putting the weight of your own body upon him.

As a result, because of the weight of your body, he will be unable to remain standing. He will thus be thrown on his back (See Fig. 43).

Fig. 43 *Kouchi-gari* No. I (2)

No. II. Assume that both contestants are in the right natural standing posture.

Assume further that you sweep your opponent's left foot with your left foot when his left leg threatens to step forward. Push up his right elbow with your left arm and at the same time, pull your right arm directly downward.

In addition, the following may also be effective: with your right arm pull his body down by pushing your right hand under his left armpit; at the same time, with your left hand push his right shoulder downward.

MAIN POINT:

Pull both hands downward and sweep his foot with fast footwork. If you push his body upward with both hands and sweep his foot also upward, you will be opening yourself to an attack by *Ko-uchi-gari-gaeshi* (revenging on *Ko-uchi-gari*). We shall describe this later.

68

How to escape:

When you are threatened with attack using this technique, pull your both arms downward by bending your own body forward. This will render the technique ineffective.

When your opponent attempts to apply this technique by pushing your body far in front or when he attacks you with it by turning his body to the side (lateral attack), turn his body to your left with both arms. Thus, only by using such action as this (i.e., turning round the body of the opponent to your left), you can free yourself.

Ko-uchi-gari-gaeshi (revenging against *Ko-uchi-gari*)

When your right foot is swept off the mat, use it in turn to sweep your opponent's left foot on which he now stands and at the same time, draw both your hands sharply to the right. He will in consequence be easily thrown. Such technique is called *Ko-uchi-gari*-gaeshi (Revenging against *Ko-uchi-gari*).

Oh-uchi-gari

In employing this technique in the right natural standing posture, allow your opponent to step forward with his left leg so as to force him to stand side by side with both feet.

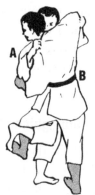

Fig. 44 *Oh-uchi-gari*

When his left foot is about to be place upon the mat (the weight of his body is at this instant being lightly supported upon the mat by this foot), with the body lowered put your left foot between his two legs by turning it to your left, and move close to him (See Fig. 44).

With your right foot sweep his left leg from the inside outward, in a motion describing a circle. Quickly then bend your own body forward and to your right, push up his right elbow with your left hand, pulling with the other hand directly downward. Thus you drop him to his left and back.

If he retreats, quickly move your own left leg forward by hooking his left leg with your right leg. At the same time, by pushing his belly with your head at the level of his front belt so as to place the weight of your body upon him, push to his left and back. The opponent (B) will then be thrown on his back.

In addition, when both contestants are separated to a certain extent, step far to the front and hook your right leg around his left leg. Quickly, with both hands, push his body down and to his left and back. In this way, you cannot be attacked afterward by the back-technique (retaliation technique), and you will still be in a position to apply this technique successfully.

70

When two contestants are separated to a medium extent or are standing in close together, by placing your left foot close to your own right heel sweep his left foot with your right leg in a manner similar to the above-mentioned movement.

Main points and how to connect this technique with *Ko-uchi-gari*:

(1) Force your opponent to place the weight of his body upon his left leg.

Note carefully: When you attack by using *Ko-uchi-gari* with your right foot, and it fails, quickly switch to *Oh-uchi-gari*, using the same foot.

When you employ this approach, you are likely to be successful, i.e., in an effort to escape from *Ko-uchi-gari*, your opponent will surely put the weight of his body on the other leg. As a result, his posture will become more vulnerable to attack by *Oh-uchi-gari*.

(2) Moving close to your opponent, promptly bend your body forward by pushing him down.

At the same time, with your right foot sweep his left leg downward in a movement describing a circle. This is the crux of the hold. Contrarywise, if you push your opponent upward and sweep his leg also upward, the weight of his body will surely be placed upon his right leg. Subsequently, you can escape by drawing back.

How to free yourself and take revenge against this technique:

When your opponent attacks you with this technique, bend your own body forward, pulling your both hands downward. Thus, you defend yourself.

Or, promptly force out his foot by holding your left leg upward. Then drop him by turning his body to your right.

In addition to this, when you are being attacked with this technique, quickly push him with your both arms and at the same time, sweeping his right foot, the one with which he is attacking you. Thus, your opponent will be dropped by counterattack.

71

Hiza-guruma

No. I. (Attack against your opponent's front-placed leg.)

Assume that both contestants are in the right natural standing posture; with the intention of forcing your opponent to walk, pull him forward.

At this moment, if you can't force him to walk forward because of his resistance, then suddenly pull him a little directly forward, moving your right foot outward and in front of his left foot about five or six inches. Pushing his body to the side with your right hand and drawing him to the left with your left hand, pull downward and to his right and front.

At the same time, stretch your left leg straight as a pole, putting the cavity of your sole upon the outside of his right knee; then turning your body to the left, pull your left arm strongly so as to make it parallel with your belt (See Fig. 45)

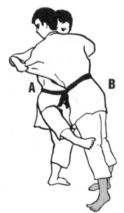

Fig. 45 *Hiza-guruma* **No. I**

At this juncture, your opponent is propped up at his right knee with your left foot; his body will be pulled sideway.

Finally, unable to hold his body in the standing position, he will then be dropped down to his right and front in a circular motion, like a wheel, with your left leg acting as an axis.

72

No. II. (Attack your opponent's back-placed leg).

In using the right natural standing posture for this tactic: change your grip from collar ("*eri*") to sleeve, i.e., pass over his left arm, grasp the middle outside part of his left sleeve with your right hand so as to embrace his left arm. Throw him off balance to his left and front by pulling him a little forward and with your left hand push his right elbow directly sideway (See: *How to disturb your opponent's balance No. 7, page 15*). Similarly, as in No. I above, prop the outside part of his left knee with your right foot (cavity of sole) and turning your body to the right, pull your right arm tightly in parallel with your own belt, taking advantage of the opportunity when the opponent threatens to drop down to his left and front (See Fig. 46).

He will thus be thrown down.

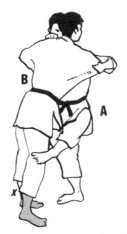

Fig. 46 *Hiza-guruma* **No. II**

MAIN POINTS:

(1) The actions of your both arms must be completely harmonized.

(2) Stretch out rigidly the leg with which you prop up his knee.

How to escape from this hold:

Push your opponent directly back so that his hips lose their balance and stability.

Thereafter, he cannot apply this technique against you.

73

Ko-soto-gari

Ko-soto-gari No. I. Assume that you sweep your opponent's foot with your own right foot.

Do this in using this technique in the natural standing posture or in the right natural standing posture: grip the upper inside part of your opponent's sleeves with each of your hands (it may also be effective to grasp the middle sleeve with your left hand), with the intention of forcing your opponent to step with his right leg (when he begins to step with his right leg after stepping with his left one); then pull your own left arm inward. Then he will surely thrust his right foot further inside (See: *How to disturb your opponent's balance No. 6, Page 14*).

Fig. 47 *Ko-soto-gari* No. I

At this instant, place your right foot in front of his left foot. Then stoop low (bending your knees with the body raised), draw your right arm inward and lift his right arm by pushing your left hand under his right armpit (when gripping the middle sleeve, push up his elbow joint) in order to break his balance to his left and back. Move close to him until you touch his lower belly: with your right foot (formed into the shape to a reaping-hook) or with your right heel. sweep the upper part of his left heel from the outside (See Fig. 47).

At the same time, lifting him up, push him with both hands to his left and back.

Then his body will be straightened and lifted in that direction.

Consequently, he will be thrown down as easily as slapping down a plate.

Ko-soto-gari No. II. In employing the natural standing posture with this hold, do this: pass over his left arm, then grasp the upper outside part of his left sleeve with your right hand so as to take hold of his left arm.

With your left hand grip the lower part of his right elbow.

74

Pull your right hand forward, then move your left leg to the left of him about one foot outward by turning around yourself to your left so as to stand side by side with him.

While pulling your left arm, push him up with your left hand in an effort to destroy his balance in the direction of his back.

Fig. 48 *Ko-soto-gari* No. II

At the same time, sweep his left heel toward the toes with your right foot. He will thus be dropped directly on his back (See Fig. 48).

At this moment, you may also attack, using this technique, by dropping yourself on your back ("*Sutemi*").

MAIN POINTS:

(1) In using No. I: move up close to him and push him, lifting him up. Pull both hands around as if you were about to draw a large circle.

(2) In using No. II: embrace his left arm with your right arm, then promptly pull him tightly forward and move your left foot to the outside of his left foot.

How to escape from this hold:

In countering against either No. I or No. II, with your body bent forward, strain hard with your both hands against him to prevent him from moving up close to you.

Then release his foot. Or this may also be a good chance to attack him with ashi-barai-gaeshi (revenging on ashi-barai).

75

Oh-soto-gari

No. I. In using this technique in the case of the right natural standing posture when both contestants are moving about, do this:

As his right foot is about to touch the mat after stepping forward, put the weight of your body upon your left leg, then move your left foot to the outside of his right leg by standing on your toes (See the above-mentioned fundamental movement).

Pull your left arm to your own right armpit, lifting him up with your right arm; then push him to his back by means of harmonized movement of your left arm. (See: *How to disturb your opponent's balance No. 8, page 15*).

Fig. 49 *Oh-soto-gari* No. I

Then push him down and to his right and back. With the body bent forward, sweep his right leg toward the toes, sliding your right foot stiffly across the mat with your right toes. Your opponent will then be dropped on his back. (See Fig. 49).

No. II. By means of the method on *How to disturb your opponent's balance No. 8, page 15*, do this: when your adversary moves to his right as a result of your pulling action, sweep his right leg by making his body unstable to his back, similar in movement to that of No. I.

No. III. Here we shall describe the technique which is applied from the right side of your opponent.

Before his left foot is placed upon the mat, by pulling him forward turn him slightly inward in an effort to pull him with your right hand. (See: *How to disturb your opponent's balance No. 8, page 15*). At this juncture, your opponent will be obliged to stand with his right leg only while holding his left leg upward.

By pulling him downward to his right and back, place your left foot close to the outside of his right leg. At the same time, sweep his right leg with your own right leg in a manner similar to No. I above. Your opponent will thus be thrown for a fall in manner as if he were drawing a large circle (See Fig. 50).

76

Fig. 50 *Oh-soto-gari* No. III

Note: In this case, it is not always easy to sweep off his foot toward the toes, so it may also be a good approach to sweep his foot directly backward.

No. IV. This is the most appropriate movement for pulling your opponent down so that you can apply this technique in a most successful way.

The method for breaking your opponent's balance should be done as follows: First, to the side, secondly in the forward direction, and finally backward.

Thus, your technique should change directions three times one after another. (See: *How to disturb your opponent's balance No. 8, page 15*).

When you attempt to disturb his balance to his right, your opponent will surely react by drawing his body back to his left in order to avoid being pushed off balance. At this moment, by lifting him up to his front with your right hand, place your left foot near the outside of his right leg, turning your own body around to his right side. And then pull him down from front to his left and front by drawing him to your right.

Apply this technique against him in a manner similar to that used in No. II above.

No. V. When your opponent begins to step back with his left leg after having stepped back with his right leg (pushed slightly so as to step back a little), you pull him down on his back by stepping up with your left leg and

77

pushing his neck forcibly to his back (or embracing his neck) with your right arm.

While he is stepping back with his left leg, by pushing his body to your left with your right hand force him to stand with his right leg alone, and without allowing his left foot to touch the mat.

Then throw him down by the above-mentioned technique.

This technique must be used only by such skillful player as one who can move his foot quickly as a flash of lightning. For this reason, it will be too difficult to use this technique among beginners.

MAIN POINTS:

(1) Lifting up your opponent, push his body with your right arm as if it were about to draw a large circle in the sky (except No. 5).

The actions of your both hands and legs must he completely harmonized.

(2) In employing techniques No. 3 and No. 4, don't loosen the action of your left hand while acting with your right one, otherwise this technique is likely to fail.

How to escape:

(1) When you are attacked by this technique, turn your opponent forcibly to your right with both hands (pull your right hand. downward and strain hard against him with your left hand so as to act as if you were about to draw an arc using both hands). At the same time, release his right foot by lifting up your own right foot to your left and front.

He will thus be dropped or he will slip and fall forward or outward.

(2) If you get an inkling that he is about to attack, rapidly move your right foot to the back, straining hard against his body with both hands.

(3) Revenge against this technique of *Oh-soto-gari*: This device of counterattack is called oh-soto-gaeshi.

78

Oh-soto-guruma

When your opponent steps back with his right leg, by striding with your right leg as if it were about to rub his right foot, pull your hand to your own left as if drawing a large circle.

His body will thus be flipped down with the motion of a mill-wheel.

Oh-soto-otoshi

Instead of sweeping his foot in attacking with *Oh-soto-gari*, put your foot deeply behind him so as to make him unable to release his leg. And then drop him on his back. Including *Oh-soto-guruma*, this technique is one of the modifications of *Oh-soto-gari* (See Fig. 51).

Fig. 51 *Oh-soto-otoshi*

Tomoe-nage

No. I (Technique to throw your opponent down directly forward over your own head).

When he takes his self-defensive posture from the front, this is the most appropriate occasion to apply this technique against him. Therefore, with each contestant taking hold in the right natural standing posture, do this: with your right hand grip his middle left sleeve by shifting the grip from his left collar ("*eri*"). Then pull him forward so as to make his both legs stand side by side. (See: *How to disturb the opponent's balance No. 5, page 14*).

Then pull him (B) down directly forward. At the same time, placing your left leg deeply between both his legs, lay yourself on your back, shifting your body into the shape of a ball.

With your right knee bent, put the sole of your right foot against his lower belly and then pull your both hands upward, stretching them out as if you were about to draw a large circle over your head. Thereby, with the aid of your stretched-out right knee, pull with your both hands strongly.

He will thus be thrown down over your head (See Fig. 52).

Fig. 52 *Tomoe-nage*

No. II (Technique to throw opponent down forward and to his side corner over your own head).

In the case of attacking with this technique, in his effort to escape his opponent he will surely turn himself a somersault by putting his right hand

80

upon the mat. When he does this, push away his right hand with your own left hand, then throw him down to his right and front.

When you want to throw him down to his left and front, use the technique in a manner just the opposite to the above-mentioned method.

When you become so skillful in the use of this technique that you can also apply it with only one hand, then do this: with the other hand push away the hand with which he attempts to turn himself a somersault for the purpose of escaping. Using either the right hand or the left, pull and haul him about vigorously, finally throwing him down forward and to his side, making a feint in the meanwhile to fool him. This technique will then be fully successful.

MAIN POINTS:

(1) Forcing him to stoop low, roll yourself on your back, in a sliding motion. Then pull him With both your hands; especially pull him tightly with the hand which is on the same side as that of your leg that is pushed up against his lower abdomen.

(2) In any technique, the action of hands and legs must be completely harmonized. Especially, in this technique, don't pull the hand or stretch out the leg too hastily, otherwise he will not be thrown. To repeat, pull your hands upward so high that when his face passes over your own, your leg is perfectly straight and his body tightly pulled toward you.

How to escape:

When you are attacked by this technique by means of your opponent's right leg, quickly turn yourself to your right, pushing away his right leg toward the inside from the outside with your left hand.

In this way you can escape, rendering this technique non-effective because of the release of his right leg.

In addition, when you are attacked with this technique, by standing with one knee push out your own lower belly and throw out your chest. Thus you can free yourself.

81

Tai-otoshi

No. I. In using this technique in the right natural standing posture while both contestants are walking, do this:

When your opponent steps forward with his left leg or when his left leg begins to follow after his back-placed right leg, with your right hand that is gripping his left collar (*"eri"*) pull his body toward the inside by turning your own right arm and with your left hand that is gripping his right sleeve, then pull his body a little so as to restrain the turning of his body to his right and back. Thus disturbing his balance to his right and front, you then step with your right leg to the outside of his right foot, putting the weight of your body upon it (don't hook your right leg around his right leg).

Then pull your opponent tightly with your left arm so as to draw an arc with your left hand (See Fig. 53).

Fig. 53 *Tai-otoshi*

In addition to this movement, with your right arm push him forcibly as if your right hand was rushing after the other hand.

Thereby, his body will be rolled down forward, your right leg acting as a fulcrum.

No. II. This technique differs from No. I in the way it disturbs your opponent's balance.

When your opponent begins to step with his right leg, by pulling his body inward with your left hand, let him step with his right foot more inside than

82

that of the common run (See: *How to disturb your opponent's balance No. 6, page 14*).

Quickly, pull up your opponent to his right and front with your right hand. And then, pull him down strongly forcing him to put the weight of his body upon his right leg. Thus, spin him down in a manner similar to No. I. In this case, the left arm should be pulled more directly downward than in No. I.

MAIN POINT:

The action to disrupt your opponent's balance is the most essential point. Therefore, you must be extra careful regarding the method you use to disturb his balance.

How to escape and how to apply the retaliation technique.

(1) When you are attacked with this technique, jump over your opponent's right leg, with your own right leg to the right. The attacking technique will then be rendered non-effective.

(2) When you are attacked by this technique, turn yourself to the right, then turn his body to the right (pull his body directly downward with both your hands as if you were drawing an arc).

Your opponent will then be dropped forward as the result of your dodging.

Uki-otoshi

The classical form of *Uki-otoshi* (original form of *Uki-otoshi*) is too theoretical for ready explanation. Therefore, here we shall describe only the form which enables you to apply it against your opponent in a practical way. Several names are given to this technique, but it will be of no consequence which form of *Uki-otoshi* you use.

Two methods are explained as follows:

Uki-otoshi No. I (Method to disturb your opponent's balance directly sideway).

Assume that your opponent is either in the natural standing posture or the right natural standing posture.

With your right hand grip his middle left sleeve (inside part) and with the other hand grasp his middle right sleeve (outside part). Now assume that both contestants are moving, appraising each other.

When he begins to step in front with his left leg after he has placed his right leg on the mat, pull your right arm inward, then he will surely place his left foot further inside than ordinarily. (See: *How to disturb your opponent's balance No. 6, page 14*).

At the same time, make a feint as if you were about to step back with your right leg, but instead move your right foot directly sideway.

Stoop low (slightly bending your knees with the body raised), then push him up to your right with your left hand in order to put the weight of his body upon his left leg.

Thus throw him off balance to his side. With your right arm, pull his body directly downward and to the right so as to push away his left arm to the outside.

84

Fig. 54 *Uki-otoshi* No. I

Your opponent will then be thrown sideway on his back as if describing a circle (See Fig. 54).

No. II. (Throwing your opponent down to his back).

In using this technique in the right natural standing posture and both contestants are walking and moving, do this: When your opponent steps back with his left leg, follow after his left leg stepping to the outside of it with your own right leg. With your right arm pull him down to his left and back and with your left arm push up his right elbow in an effort to disturb his balance to his left and back. Then throw him down to his left and back in a manner similar to that used in No. I.

In addition, when he steps forward with his right leg, pull your own left arm and push up his body and then attack him with this technique similarly as in above-mentioned movement.

MAIN POINT:

The movements for disturbing your opponent's balance are the essential point. Namely, when his hip inclines to the outside of the vertical line running through the outside of his left foot, apply this technique quickly. He will then be successfully vanquished.

A point to note: Harmony of movements for spreading the legs, pulling the hands and carrying the body is a vital part of this technique.

Move close to your opponent, otherwise you will fail in the use of this technique.

How to escape:

Move your hips back in order to separate yourself from your opponent. Strain hard against his body with both hands. Take careful note: if you can jump over with your left leg, you will not be thrown down.

85

Yoko-gake

No. I (Technique to throw your opponent using a large motion).

In using this technique in the right natural standing posture, do this: push his body to his right and back. Then using the energy he exerts in trying to draw back, pull him down to his right and front. Thus his body will become off balance; consequently, he will attempt to thrust his right leg far forward.

At this moment, place your right foot in front of his left foot and drop on your back to the right and back by turning around to your left.

With your left foot strained, prop it against the lower part of his right leg that is about be to be placed upon the mat after he has stepped far forward. In this manner, throw him down to his right and front, using of the force engendered when you drop yourself on your back and pull with your both hands. At this stage, he will be thrown over your head, in a movement resembling an arc in the sky, and ending with a straight line with your body (See. Fig. 55).

Fig. 55 *Yoko-gake*

Note: when throwing him down, push both hands high upward, as if drawing a large circle over your own left shoulder, crossing both hands over your own head.

Your opponent will then be thrown down on his back instead of dropping on his side.

No. II. (Technique to throw your opponent down by a medium motion).

When your opponent is in the natural standing posture (standing with the two feet side by side) or when he has given up his mind to step with his

86

right leg right in the middle of his stepping as a result of being pulled down, place your right foot close to the outside of his left foot.

Then turn your body a little to the left. Now drop yourself upon your left shoulder keeping your right shoulder upward. Thus, apply this technique similarly as in No. 1. Now, in the case of No. 1, keep your right shoulder a little upward without allowing your back to touch tightly upon the mat.

No. III (Technique to throw your opponent down by a small motion).

Two methods used are as follows:

(1) In applying this technique in the right natural standing posture while both contestants are walking and moving, do this: while your opponent begins to step forward with his right leg after stepping with his left foot, pull your left hand a little inward, then he will be obliged to place his right foot further inside than in the case of the common run (See: *How to disturb your opponent's balance, No. 6, page 14*). At this stage, push your opponent's body to the side with your right arm, pulling him directly downward with your left arm; then sweep his right ankle-bone directly side-way with your stretched left leg. At the same time, turn your body to the left, drop yourself on your left side. You thus throw him down on his right.

(2) This technique is employed against his leg which stood behind his other leg.

In applying the technique in the right natural standing posture, do this: with your right hand grip the middle outside part of your opponent's left sleeve, changing your grip from his left collar (*"eri"*); then by means of the method How to disturb your opponent's balance, No. 7 (*See page 14*) draw him down forward and to his left. At the same time, pull the body of your opponent with your right hand, placing your left foot in front of his right foot. And then, drop yourself on your right side so as to make your body into the shape of a hook (the shape of a Japanese syllable<), rolling with his body.

By sweeping the lower part of his left leg with right foot, throw him down to his left and front similarly as in No. II.

Incidentally, this technique is so dangerous for *Judo* trainees that it should be employed only by the skillful player.

87

Therefore, beginners should concentrate on being proficient in the techniques No. I and No. II.

MAIN POINTS:

(1) How to disrupt your opponent's balance is the essential point. Therefore, you are required to train thoroughly in the above-mentioned art of destroying his balance.

When your opponent's hip is inclined to the outside of a vertical line running through the outside of his foot, this technique can usually be executed successfully. Note carefully: this maneuver for disturbing your opponent's balance should be done perfectly, so as to be ready immediately afterward for attacking with this above-mentioned technique.

(2) Drop your body together with your opponent.

(3) Put strength and tension on your foot, shoving it forward. Standing on your toes, raise your hips and push out your lower belly and then turn the body by drawing in both hands strongly.

At the last moment, pull him so as to cross both your hands.

How to escape:

Jump over the foot of your adversary that threatens to impede your leg. Thus you can escape from this hold.

Kata-guruma

Assume that both contestants are in the right natural standing posture: Gripping the inside part of your opponent's right cuff with your left hand, pull him to his right and front. At the same time, stooping low, put your own right shoulder tightly against his right thigh. Then from inside his right thigh embrace his right thigh with your right arm.

Then by pulling his right arm downward with your left hand and lifting up his body with your right arm, quickly raise yourself up so as to lift up his body upon your shoulder.

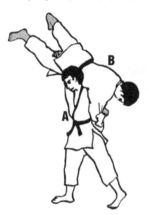

Fig. 56 *Kata-guruma*

Thus, throw your opponent (B) down directly forward or to the left and front by moving your left leg close to your right leg (See Fig. 56).

MAIN POINT:

Tightly pull his body with your left arm and put your shoulder deeply against his thigh.

How to escape:

Retreat with your left foot, turn yourself to the left and push down his neck with your right hand. Or, promptly put your right knee on the mat. In addition, tense your both legs as you lean forward, embracing his neck with your both arms so that you are ready to attack with Okuri-eri-jime technique either from his front or back. Also, when he pushes his arm between your thighs attempting an eri-brace, seize the attacking arm tightly between your thighs in order to counterattack with sankaku-gatame (Triangle hold) or ude-hishigi-tai-gatame.

89

Tsuri-goshi

"*Ko*" means small.

"*Oh*" means large.

We can divide this hold into two parts as follows: *Oh*(large)-*tsuri-goshi* and *Ko*(small)-*tsuri-goshi*.

(1) *Oh-tsuri-goshi*

Over the shoulder of your opponent, gripping his back belt and lifting him up, throw him down similarly as in *Uki-goshi* by placing your hip against him.

(2) *Ko-tsuri-goshi*

Under the armpit of your opponent, grip his back belt. The rest of the movement can be the same as for the above-mentioned hold.

Sumi-taoshi

Both contestants are in the right self-defensive posture.

Sumi-taoshi No. I. When you attempt to pull your opponent down to his right and front, in a defensive reaction he is certain to draw his body back. Taking advantage of this opportunity, move in the contrary direction, pulling him down to his right and back.

Placing your right foot close in front of his right foot, put the sole of your own left foot upon his right heel and drop down yourself to your left and front by placing the weight of your body upon your left leg. The opponent will then be thrown down to his right and back.

No. II. When you draw your opponent to his left and front, he will surely react by stepping forward with his left foot. At this stage, with the right arm push his body to his right and back before he has a chance to place his left leg on the mat. Then stepping forward, and with your left arm, pull him downward in your effort to break his balance to his right and back. Next throw him down in a manner similar to No. I above. (See Fig. 57).

Fig. 57 *Sumi-taoshi* No. II

As one of the leading movements for attacking by *Katame-waza* (Locking technique), this movement is very useful.

Therefore, it is often practised in the *Kite-ryu* (another school of *Judo*) in conjunction with *Yoko-gake.*

91

Sumi-gaeshi

In employing this technique in the right self-defensive posture, carry out these movements: By drawing your opponent forcibly to his right and front, put your left foot to the inside of his right leg; then with the aid of your right hand pull his body tightly with your left hand while lying yourself on your back.

Put your right instep under the back of his left knee; kick his body up. The opponent will thus be thrown to his right and front above. (See Fig. 58).

Fig. 58 *Sumi-gaeshi*

Though this hold is justifiably considered as one of the effective throwing techniques, you should not be charmed by spectacular success in the use of it but you should regard it only as one of the leading movements for attacking with *Katame-waza* (Locking technique), since this technique is very useful.

Yoko-guruma

When you are threatened with an attack by means of a throwing technique from your right side, counter with these moves: With the hips lowered embrace your opponent's hip from his back with your left arm, and holding his lower abdomen with your right arm, throw him by using the revenging technique (for instance, *Ura-nage*). Then he is certain to bend his body forward trying to free himself.

At this stage, with your left hand push his body forward by thrusting your own left arm until it is placed upon his back. His balance will then be disrupted in his front. Promptly, turning around to his right side, slip your own right leg between his legs by dropping yourself to his right and front. Make use of the energy engendered by the drop of your body, throwing him over your own body to his right and front.

Daki-wakare

When you are attacked by a throwing technique, you must counter by throwing your opponent down with *Ushiro-goshi* or *Ura-nage*. At this stage, it so happens that he will crawl on all fours with his body bent forward, trying to evade your hold.

So now you attack him: Embracing your opponent's hips, throw him in the opposite direction to that in which he expects to be thrown, doing this by means of running on to the right and left promptly so as to make a feint, as if you were about to throw him down to the side he is expecting.

For instance: Assume that you move rapidly to his left side from the right. Put your left leg inside of his left leg from the outside. Taking advantage of the momentum engendered by the action of rushing in, lift up his body with your both arms (See Fig. 59).

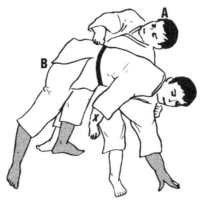

Fig. 59 *Daki-wakure*

At the same time, drop yourself on your side, and throw him over your right shoulder.

Note: when embracing his hip, if possible, grip his collar (*"eri"*) with one hand. This will give you a tighter attack.

94

Tawara-gaeshi

This technique is much the same in principle as throwing a straw-bag down after carrying it on your shoulder.

Incidentally, you embrace his body directly from the front, opposite from the direction employed in *Daki-wakare*.

In this case, push his head with your lower abdomen, then lift up his body with both arms. At the same time, drop yourself on your back, throw him over your head.

Uki-waza

In employing this technique in the right self-defensive posture, do this: Step back with your right leg, pull your opponent to his front with your both arms, assisted by your body, in an effort of disturb his balance to his left and front, forcing him to step forward with his left leg. Then move your left leg back, drop yourself on your back.

Taking advantage of the energy engendered by this dropping action, throw him to his right and front (i.e. your own left and back corner).

Note this: At the start, pull him to his left and front, secondly draw him down to his right and front. He will then be easily and perfectly removed off balance.

Besides all this, we might mention the following other techniques: i.e., so-called *Yoko-otoshi, Obi-otoshi, Tani-otoshi, Kuchiki-taoshi, Hikkomi-gaeshi, Yoko-wakare* and *Yama-arashi*, etc.

These latter throwing techniques are not only too theoretical for practical use but no one would be charmed by any spectacular attraction. Because of this fact, it would be useless to describe them here in detail.

CHAPTER IV
How to attack your opponent by changing techniques one after the other

In a match, you are always required to be so skillful in the art that you can apply the techniques freely and reflexively at any time.

In the process of making yourself a skillful *Judo* player, you must train yourself thoroughly in the method of how to shift your technique for the most appropriate one by taking advantage of your opponent's disrupted posture (the opponent himself will also disturb his balance as a result of his struggles), all this while he is using his attacking technique. Meanwhile, you should practise various methods of attack by going over them continuously over and over again, from first to the last.

Such attacking method with which we are here concerned is much more effective than using the fragmented movements technique. Therefore, you must practise these techniques parallel with the ones which are your favourite, intending to make yourself a master of them.

Accordingly, the above-mentioned "fundamental principles of *Judo* training and method" are considered to be necessary for *Judo* trainees.

Several methods used are as follows: How to attack your opponent by changing your technique for the appropriate one while engaged in offensive tactics.

When you fail in the use of one technique, promptly attack him again by using the same technique or using any other one against him in conjunction with both types of technique employing them smoothly one after the other.

To recapitulate, when you fail to thrown him to his front, quickly attack him and throw him to the opposite (back) side. In using a technique to throw him backward, if this fails, as soon as possible resume the attack and throw him to his front.

When you fail to throw him to his right, promptly attack him again and throw him to his left.

1. How to switch to *Seoi-nage* from *Ko-soto-gari*.

97

Assume that both contestants are in the right natural standing posture.

Use *Ko-soto-gari* against your opponent's left leg with your own right foot. If this fails because he is able to get away, promptly attack by means of *Seoi-nage* from his right.

2. How to switch to *Seoi-nage* from *Oh-soto-gari*.

Attack with *Oh-soto-gari* against his right leg. If you are threatened to be attacked by means of the revenging technique of this hold, quickly turn your body and with seoi-nage, using it from his right, to throw him down.

3. How to switch to *Seoi-nage* or *Tsurikomi-goshi* from *Tai-otoshi*.

If you fail in the use of *Tai-otoshi* against your opponent is right side, quickly attack him with *Seoi-nage* or *Tsurikomi-goshi* from his right.

4. How to switch to *Harai-goshi* from *Tai-otoshi*.

When you fail in the use of *Tai-otoshi* against his right side, leave your right leg in the same position as before and attack him with *Harai-goshi* from his left.

5. How to switch to *Maki-komi* from *Hane-goshi*.

Attack by *Hane-goshi*. If it fails, or if your first intention to grapple him by *Maki-komi* is unsuccessful. Attack him with *Soto-maki-komi* (above described *Hane-maki-komi*) by switching to this technique from *Hane-goshi*.

6. How to switch to *Hane-goshi* from *Ko-soto-gari*.

Attack with *Ko-soto-gari* against his left foot with your own right foot. If he escapes, attack him with *Hane-goshi* from his right side, promptly striking with your left leg.

7. Attack him by shifting your technique from *Oh-uchi-gari* for *Uchi-mata*, or attack with *Oh-uchi-gari* from his right side. If he escapes by bending his body forward, attack him with *Uchi-mata* on his right side, rushing into him.

Again, when you fail with *Uchi-mata*, promptly attack him by means of *Oh-uchi-gari*, using the same foot.

8. How to switch to *Tomoe-nage* from *Ko-uchi-gari*.

98

Attack with *Ko-uchi-gari*. If he tries to escape by bending his body forward, take advantage of his pulled-down posture and attack by *Tomoe-nage* with the other foot thrust far forward, making use of the leg with which you attacked using *Ko-uchi-gari*, placing it against your opponent.

9. How to switch to *Tomoe-nage* from *Oh-uchi-gari*.

For instance: Attack by *Oh-uchi-gari* against your opponent's right foot with your left leg. If he escapes, use *Tomoe-nage* with your right foot by stepping up far forward with the left leg.

10. How to switch to *Oh-uchi-gari* from *Ko-uchi-gari*.

For example: Attack by *Ko-uchi-gari* against his right foot with your right foot. If he escapes, throw him down by *Oh-uchi-gari* against his left foot, making use of your same foot. If he places the weight of his body upon one leg, with the intention of escaping from your *Ko-uchi-gari* technique, his posture will then become suitable for your attack by *Oh-uchi-gari*.

11. How to switch to *Ko-uchi-gari* from *Uchi-mata*.

Use *Uchi-mata* for attack on his right thigh. If it fails. promptly attack him with *Ko-uchi-gari*, using the same foot against his right foot. This technique is so effective that you can win even though you may be fighting against great odds.

12. How to switch to *Oh-soto-gari* from *Okuri-ashi-barai* or *De-ashi-barai*.

If you fail in delivering *Okuri-ashi-barai* or *De-ashi-barai* by using your left foot against his right foot, then promptly attack him with *Oh-soto-gari*. With your right leg take advantage of his pulled-down posture, lift his left foot but leaving his right leg in the same position.

13. How to switch to *Oh-soto-gari* from *Ko-soto-gari*.

Attack by means of *Ko-soto-gari* against your opponent's left foot with your right foot. If he escapes, quickly attack him by using *Oh-soto-gari* against his right leg with your same foot.

14. How to switch to *Uchi-mata* from *Tsurikomi-ashi*.

Attack by means of *Tsurikomi-ashi* with your left foot. If he jumps over your left foot with his right leg in an effort to escape, promptly attack him with *Uchi-mata* against his right thigh, rushing into him.

15. How to attack with *Tsurikomi-ashi* on the right and left sides in rapid succession.

As soon as you fail to deliver *Tsurikomi-ashi* against his right foot, attack him with the same technique against his other foot (his left foot) in rapid succession.

16. How to switch to *Harai-goshi* from *De-ashi-barai*.

When you fail to deliver *De-ashi-barai* against his left foot, quickly attack him with *Harai-goshi* on his right side.

17. How switch to *Katame-waza* (locking technique) from *Tomoe-nage*.

Throw him down by *Tomoe-nage*, attack him with *Ude-hishigi-juji-gatame* or by other *Katame-waza*, taking advantage of the energy engendered when you drop yourself on your back.

18. How to switch to *Katame-waza* from *Yoke-gake, Sumi-taoshi* or *Sumi-gaeshi*.

Use such technique as *Sutemi-waza* (throwing your opponent down by dropping yourself with him). Switching from *Yoko-gake, Sumi-taoshi* or *Sumi-gaeshi*, attack him with *Katame-waza*, getting up yourself quickly before he rises up.

Rising to your feet, pull his arm upward with one hand and at the same time push his other armpit with your foot (use the foot on the side opposite to your pulling hand), or place your knee upon his belly in order to restrain his movements.

By these numerous switches of techniques employed one after the other in rapid succession, throw him down or lock him securely in conjunction with *Katame-waza*.

How to throw your opponent down in conjunction with his own technique.

100

Methods on how to connect your opponent's technique with your own while attacking him may be described as follows:

Taking advantage of your opponent's pulled-down posture resulting from your attacking technique, you employ a suitable technique against him picked according to his posture and the technique he is using.

1. When he attacks you with a technique, take advantage of the energy engendered by the motion of the technique he uses, then throw him down by a sliding motion. Such technique as this one is generally called *Sukashi-waza* (throwing your opponent by sliding him out), and it is one of the modifications of *Uki-otoshi*.

For example: the above described "How to escape from *Oh-soto-gari* (1)" and "How to escape from *Uchi-mata*" may be explained further:

2. Escape from your opponent's technique so very quickly that you can apply an appropriate counter-technique against him according to the direction in which you pull him down, taking advantage of the energy engendered by use of your technique.

For example: The above-mentioned *Ashi-barai-gaeshi* (gaeshi, meaning revenging), *Ko-uchi-gari-gaeshi* and *Hane-goshi-no-gaeshi* (revenging on *Hane-goshi*) may be used.

In addition, in conjunction with your opponent's technique, deliver these holds: When he attacks you with *Oh-uchi-gari*, attack him by *Tomoe-nage*; when he attempts to throw you with *Ko-soto-gari*, attack him by *Uchi-mata*, *Harai-goshi*, *Hane-goshi* or other hip-throwing techniques. When he attacks you with *De-ashi-barai*, counterattack with *Ko-uchi-gari*.

In conclusion, I would like here to express my deep gratitude for the efforts of my special assistant, Professor Yaichibe Kanemitsu, 9th Dan, author of "*Judo no hongi*", formerly of the old Sixth High School and now director of the Genyukai Hall in Okayama.

Made in the USA
Las Vegas, NV
22 April 2024

88994658R00056